MEET THE T-REX

Fun Facts & Cool Pictures

Julian Hawking

Table of Contents

The T-Rex

Tyrannosaurus rex, or T-rex, is a dinosaur that lived many years ago and is one of the biggest meat-eating creatures that ever lived. The name *tyrannosaurus* means *tyrant lizard* and is of Greek origin, but whether this dinosaur was mean and vicious or simply a scavenger is still discussed among experts.

What kind of home did T-rex live in? Based on the location of fossil finds, experts say T-rex favored forested river lands for habitats and seem to be more populated in what is now the United States. Tyrannosaurus rex bones have been discovered in several states in the US as well as in Canada and China.

When T-rex skeletons are located, experts spend a lot of time carefully examining the bones, location, and other facts. This is so each skeleton that will be placed on display has an accurate description and reliable information for the people who come to view and learn about these big dinosaurs. Today about 30 T-rex skeletons have been found worldwide, though most are not complete.

When the T-Rex Lived

Tyrannosaurus rex lived in the late Cretaceous (sounds like cruh-tay-shus) period, a time when things were changing on the earth. By the end of this period, many of the dinosaurs, T-rex included, would no longer exist. Most scientists believe a meteor was to blame for the mass extinction.

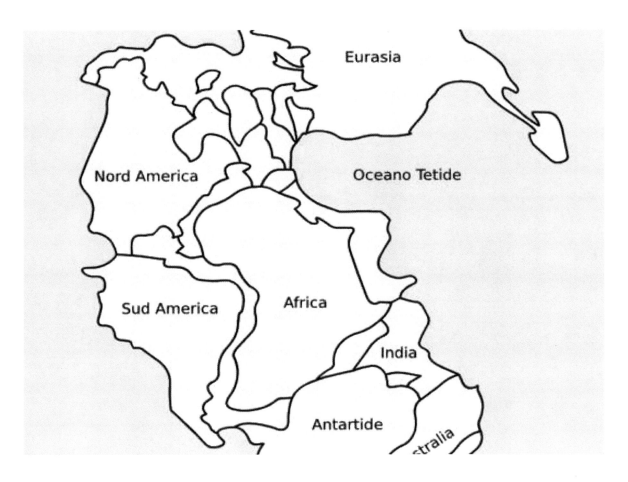

Before the meteor struck, there were many other changes taking place during the Cretaceous period. This would be the time when the land mass Pangaea (pan-gee-uh) would begin to separate into smaller land masses. This period would also experience a temperature spike and cool down, which had a significant effect on plant life and trees.

You might be surprised to learn that T-rex was not the only large meat-eating dinosaur alive during this period. Spinosaurus was equally impressive, with a huge fin along its back. The two probably never crossed paths, however, since Spinosaurus mainly lived in the South and T-rex made his home in the North. If they had met up though then this is what it might have looked like.

Anatomy of the T-Rex

T-rex was a huge beast that was at the top of the food chain during its lifetime. This was an animal whose head was nearly as big as a car; it stood about 20 feet tall. If you have an average single-story house, T-rex could have stood over your home and looked at the roof. If that isn't scary enough, you should see the size of its teeth; they were several inches long and capable of crushing scales, bones, and shells. Each T-rex had up to 60 saw-like teeth of varying sizes.

If you think Tyrannosaurus rex had impressive height, wait till you find out how long they were. A famous skeleton nicknamed Sue is about 42 feet long, which is nearly half the length of a football field. Adding to the height and length was the possible massive weight of T-rex, which experts estimate could be as much as 9 tons.

If there is one thing odd about this giant dinosaur, it is the size of its arms. When compared to the rest of the body, they are quite small, even though they are at least three feet long. Experts cannot agree on what T-rex would have used the smaller arms for; perhaps they were just for pushing off the ground if and when the large animal fell or was knocked down.

Many scientists believe birds evolved from dinosaurs or at least that the two had a common ancestor. So did T-rex have feathers? There is no proof that they did, but some suggest that evidence points to younger Tyrannosauruses possibly having feathers until they got older and no longer needed the extra warmth.

How the T-Rex Moved

If you have seen movies like *Jurassic Park*, you have seen a good description of how these dinosaurs moved. However, it is not true that T-rex had to see their prey to track it down, because they had an amazing sense of smell. For a long time people believed these dinosaurs ran upright, but due to their massive size and long tail, the forward-leaning position as seen in the movie is probably more correct.

Could T-rex run very fast? This is a question that no one has been able to answer for sure. By looking at the design of the leg bones and assuming the structure of muscles, scientists can estimate but never really know the true speed. Their top speed was somewhere between 11 and 45 miles per hour.

Another common question is whether T-rex could turn very well. Most would say no; their massive size and the manner in which they carried their body would make even a 45-degree turn slow in comparison to humans. We can make that turn in a fraction of a second, while T-rex would need a full two seconds to do the same.

Senses of the T-Rex

There is a lot of information and talk about how strong the Tyrannosaurus bite would have been and how fast they could run, but what about their other senses? How well could T-rex hear, smell, or see?

When you look at the skull of a Tyrannosaurus rex, you will find eye sockets that are a good four inches across. This tells us their eyeballs were approximately three inches in diameter and that they may have been best suited to hunting at night. Many mammalian predators with large eyes are nocturnal in nature. Further studies suggest this dinosaur may have had vision far better than hawks or even humans.

Smell is probably the sense where T-rex excelled the most. Scientists have discovered there was a large section of the brain dedicated to its sense of smell. Animals today that have such large areas dedicated to scent are animals who hunt at night over large areas and can detect prey from quite some distance.

Hearing is determined by the structure of the inner ear, and in T-rex, this structure is similar to that of animals who are much lighter and more agile. This leads experts to believe T-rex had a strong sense of hearing as well. According to internal ear structure, this dinosaur could hear low-level frequencies over long distances, allowing it to easily track prey.

T-Rex Feeding Habits

Another argument revolving around T-rex behavior is whether they were scavengers or hunters in nature. There are good arguments for both sides, but given their massive size, bone-crushing teeth, and forward-facing eyes, there is a good chance the T-rex was a very good hunter.

What did T-rex eat? There is no argument on that front: meat was always on the menu, and their diet likely consisted of triceratops, hadrosaur, behemoth, and possibly each other. It is not uncommon for large predators to make a meal of a rival they have just fought and killed.

In the end, most people agree that T-rex was an avid hunter who would also scavenge a meal when the opportunity presented itself. One thing is certain; Tyrannosaurus rex was never a vegetarian.

Sociability of T-Rexs

Did these dinosaurs stick together? Most of the evidence available says no; as a general rule, each T-rex was a loner who hunted, lived, and died alone. Of course, there have been some discoveries of multiple skeletons in the same location, which has led many to rethink the idea of the T-rex being a lone ranger.

It is possible that the Tyrannosaurus rex would team up, most often as youths, to hunt in packs and protect each other. In South Dakota, experts found three skeleton remains of this dinosaur in fairly close proximity to each other. Many began to believe this suggested the dinosaur may have buddied up at some point in their life.

Lifespan of a T-Rex

How long did these dinosaurs live? Estimates are hard to create due to the limited information available. However, when you compare them to their closest relatives, the figure tends to be approximately 20–30 years of age. This is a lot less than the estimated 80 years of similarly sized herbivores of the time.

Earliest Finds

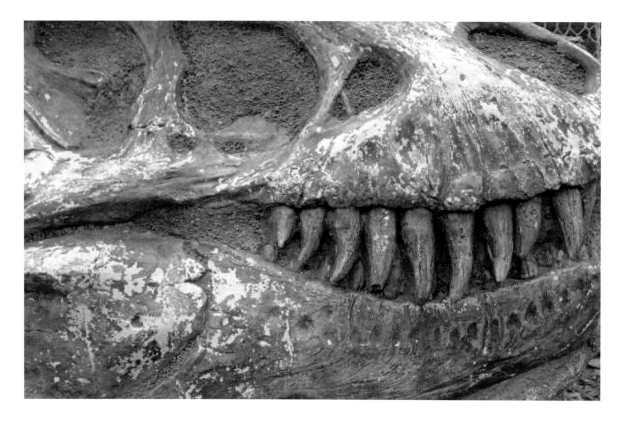

Tyrannosaurus rex skeletons have been found in North America, Canada, and China. For a long time, the earliest recorded discovery was attributed to Barnum Brown in 1902. However, teeth discovered in 1874 by Author Lakes near Golden, Colorado, are now known to be T-rex teeth, which would make them the earliest find.

Sue & Stan

(*Connie Ma*)

There have been two noteworthy T-rex finds; they've been named Sue and Stan for the amateur paleontologists who found them. Sue Hendrickson discovered the biggest and most complete skeleton to date. "Sue" is about 85 percent complete—still the most complete skeleton of a T-rex today— and even though the display has a female name, scientists are unsure whether it is a girl or boy dinosaur.

(*Ashstar01*)

Stan is a 63 percent complete skeleton that was discovered in 1987 but not collected until 1992. Originally, the bones were believed to be those of a Triceratops. During examination, Stan was found to have multiple broken and healed bones as well as a T-rex tooth-sized hole in its skull.

Weird Facts:

- At age 14, T-rex would rapidly begin putting on weight—about 1,300 pounds per year.
- Medical examiners discovered evidence of gout in the finger bones of Sue.
- T-rex only had two fingers on each "hand."

Films

Tyrannosaurus rex has been featured in several movies, including multiple cartoons. One of the most famous recent movies, and the one that shows the most accurate movements of a T-rex, is *Jurassic Park*. In this movie, scientists discovered a way to bring dinosaurs back and created an island park for visitors, until everything went wrong. Other films featuring T-rex include:

- *The Lost World*
- *Meet the Robinsons*
- *Barney and Friends*
- *The Land Before Time*

Other Books In This Series

Did you know that there are other dinosaur books in this series that you might enjoy?

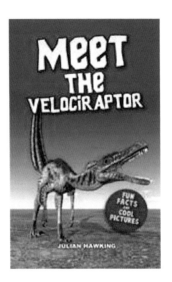

Meet The Velociraptor

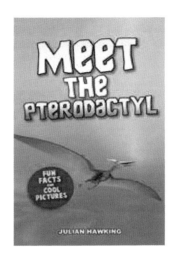

Meet The Pterodactyl

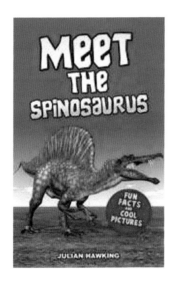

Meet The Spinosaurus

Made in the USA
Lexington, KY
27 January 2014